# TRAVELS ON A BIKE 2

## *Italy*

Garry McGivern

Cover designed by Garry McGivern

Follow Garry on social media
Visit my website at www.garrymcgivern.com

Facebook;  www.facebook.com/travelsonabike2

Instagram; www.instagram.com/garrymcgivern

YouTube; www.youtube.com/user/travelsonabike2

Twitter; www.twitter.com/GarryMcGivern

First Printing: June 2020

ISBN 9798663675734

# CONTENTS

Garry McGivern, a middle-aged, overweight widower, who drinks too much and eats too much! But who without any practice or training can ride a bike for miles! And has been bicycle touring different countries since 2008.

This is Garry's bicycle tour of Italy.

Map showing where Garry spent each night of his tour.

**Introduction**

The compulsive urge to travel is a recognised physical condition, and I'm glad to say I suffer from it! Dromomania!

After the death of my wife in 2007, I started to ride my bike and travel. Sure, there are faster and easier ways of travelling. But for me, the joy of travelling on a bicycle is uncomparable. A bicycle allows time to take in the surroundings. And with a tent on the back, I'm able to stop whenever or wherever I want!

When I embarked on my first long-distance ride in 2008. There was a lot of concern from family and friends for my safety! To put everybody at ease, I started writing a daily blog and posting it online. Which I continue to do, to this day, whenever I'm away cycling! This book is a broader version of the blogs I write each day. Recounting the highs and lows, thoughts and occurrences of life as a cycle tourist.

May 2010, after looking at a map of the world, I wondered where I could travel to this year. The choice was vast. But I was too nervous about flying, I was worried my bike might arrive damaged, or even worse, not arrive at all! So it had to be somewhere in Europe. I decided that Italy looked a great country to tour, but first I had to get there! After using trains on some of my previous trips, I consulted my Thomas Cook European train timetable. And found I could get a train from Amsterdam to Munich. Then Munich to Venice! Where I could start my tour of Italy, but first to get to Amsterdam. These are the musings I wrote as I embarked on my 3000-mile cycle ride around Italy.

# SATURDAY, 15TH MAY 2010. BOGNOR REGIS TO CAPEL LE FERNE. 110 MILES.

Well, I'm amazed at today's mileage! I thought on Thursday that I wasn't going to be able to come away! Thursday morning, I woke up in the most excruciating pain, and couldn't walk! In fact, I was in so much pain, and I ended up calling the doctor out!

After an examination, the doctor thought my sciatic nerve had gone into spasm! And told me to rest and gave me a prescription for some pain killers! Will you be able to get these yourself, asked the doctor? I just said yes, knowing it would be a big struggle! After she had left, I went to get on my bike, it was a struggle! But I managed to just about make it to the chemist. In the chemist, I had to wait for the prescription to be made up, that was agony, and I struggled to keep it together! Finally, my script was ready, and I could make the 300-metre ride home! I fell through the back door, and lay there, on the floor! I must have been there for a good hour, waiting for my tablets to kick-in!

I'm still in a lot of pain, but on my bike I'm fine, it's as though nothing is wrong. As today's mileage shows! I did, however, struggle when it came to putting my tent up, tonight! But equipped with as many painkillers, and anti-inflammatory tablets as I can carry! I'm hopeful that I'll have cycled Italy before they run out!

As you can imagine, it's been a long day, with one or two hills. And a particularly tough one right at the end of the day, coming out of Folkstone! It's only about 10-miles to the ferry terminal, in Dover. Hopefully, I'll be able to get on an early ferry, to France, tomorrow morning.

## SUNDAY, 16TH MAY. CAPEL LE FERNE TO DE HAAN, BELGIUM. 83 MILES.

At the campsite in Capel le Ferne last night, I was talking to the man in the tent next to me. He was telling me that he was in training to swim the English Channel, it's costing him nearly £3000! Not sure what the money covers, but I think it's official things. He has one week to make his attempt! His is in August. I wished him luck and retired into my tent for the night.

The ride from the campsite to the boat was all downhill, and not as far as I thought! And as planned, I managed to get on an early ferry. I was in France, by 9.30. Off the boat, I had my usual problem, of finding the right road! You have to remember, the only maps I carry, cover the whole country! As a result, there's not a great deal of detail! And every road I took seemed to lead to a motorway! Luckily an English trucker pointed me in the right direction, and it didn't take me long to cycle the 40 miles to Belgium.

Cycling in Belgium is a delight, it's all cycle paths, in fact, I don't think I've been on a single road, since arriving in Belgium! When cycle paths cross, roads, cyclists have the right of way, and cars have to stop for you! I'm not used to that!

# MONDAY, 17<sup>TH</sup> MAY. DE HAAN TO THE HOOK OF HOLLAND, HOLLAND. 118 MILES.

It rained overnight, which kept me awake for a while. But when it was time to get up, it had stopped, and the sun was shining.

I crossed the border into Holland this morning, not that I would have known it! I only realised when I caught sight of a ridiculously small sign! That was more fitting to a sign, you'd see entering a small village!

There are even more cycle paths here. Unfortunately, they don't follow the roads, which is a big problem for me! The signs on the cycle routes tend to give you the name of the next village! Which would be fine if I knew where that village was! Villages aren't marked on my maps! According to my map, there's only a handful of towns between De Haan and the Hook of Holland! So telling me that so and so is only 3kms away is no good, I need to know where the next big town is!

I cycled on a few of these routes, but found it all too frustrating! Not knowing where I was or if I was even going in the right direction! I had to keep stopping and asking for directions, thankfully most people speak good English!

Eventually, I gave up on the cycle routes and went back to cycling on the road, where I knew where I was going! That didn't go too well, either! I've never had so much abuse from motorists or anybody else! They were shouting, they were beeping! And I was a little surprised, considering they're such a cycle-friendly nation! But with such a good cycle network there's no need to be on the road. As long as you know, where you're going! Think I'd just as well throw my map away!

Because I've had to stick to cycle paths, It's been a long day, zig-zagging between towns and I didn't finish until nearly 8pm! Hopefully, tomorrow will be better!

What do you expect in Holland!

# TUESDAY, 18TH MAY. THE HOOK OF HOLLAND TO AMSTERDAM. 64 MILES.

Lovely ride this morning following the coast, cycling through the sand dunes. I enjoyed the cycle paths today! It did help that I could relate to the signs today. They had place names on them that I could see on my map!

Well, my bad leg has held out and got me as far as Amsterdam, I still can't walk on it very well, but it's perfectly okay when I'm riding. I was thinking that had my leg been hurting too much by the time I reached Amsterdam, I would give up and go home. But seeing as I'm okay cycling, I'm going to continue!

I arrived in Amsterdam just after lunch and spent the afternoon looking playing the tourist, there are thousands of bikes everywhere! I even saw a multi-storey park for bikes at the railway station!

I'm now waiting for the night train that will take me to Munich. I feel sorry for the people who end up sleeping in the same couchette as me, what with my snoring! But like the lady said when I booked the ticket "zat is not your problem!"

# WEDNESDAY, 19TH MAY. MUNICH.

I managed to get on the wrong half of the train last night! Thankfully the guard pointed it out to me. But it was just before the train was due to depart, causing me a bit of panic! The half I was on was heading to Zurich! Which is a bit out of my way? But hey, I've never been to Switzerland so it wouldn't have been all bad! With the train about to depart, I quickly loaded my bike up and headed to the other end of the train! With a fully loaded bike, a dodgy leg and a big gap between the train and platform, it was all a bit of a struggle! After my little panic, I retired to my couchette, and found that I had it to myself!

I arrived in Munich around 7.30am and went for a coffee with Anna, a girl I'd briefly met while getting from one end of the train to the other last night. She had just cycled the Rhine River and was on her way back home to northern Italy. We spent an hour or so talking before she had to catch her next train, I also had to get on!

My camera had broken when I was in Holland, and I needed to find a replacement. But more importantly, my Rohloff gear hub had sprung an oil leak! Luckily there was a cycle shop just across the road from the railway station! Even more fortunate for me! One of the mechanics had been on a Rohloff technicians course! And after looking at the gears, said it was an inner seal that needed replacing. But they couldn't fix it! Not to worry though, the hub would be okay to ride on. Even with the miles, I'm expecting to do. Apparently, the Rohloff hub would be okay to ride even if there was no oil in it at all! If that's the case, why bother putting oil in, in the first place? The technician seemed to know what he was talking about, which put me at ease!

Next on the list was a new camera, which again was a relatively easy job, the hard part was parting with the cash!

I spent the rest of the day looking around the sites of Munich, and generally hanging around until my train departs tonight at 8pm. I must admit that I've found it pretty cold today. But I think that was down to hanging around a lot!

I'm feeling more tired tonight than if I'd cycled a 100 miles!

Where's the road?

## THURSDAY, 20<sup>TH</sup> MAY. VENICE TO CASAL BORSITTA NORTH OF RAVENNA. 86 MILES.

After boarding the train last night, I checked twice, that I was on the correct part, before finding my couchette. I came up trumps again, it seems that I have a six-berth couchette all to myself! That's good. I like this overnight train travel!

My solitude didn't last long! A group of Americans joined the train in Innsbruck, which provided some amusement for me! The Americans were all rather elderly, and how can I put this, not exactly the slimmest people in the world!

As I was the first person in the carriage, I took one of the bottom bunks, leaving the Americans the remaining beds. Have you ever seen large elderly people trying to climb a ladder! Into a bunk, that was three storey's high! It didn't happen! I did offer to move so at least there was one less person that had to climb the ladder. But they declined and decided to not bother with the bunks at all, leaving me all alone once again! I was a little worried about them, but they reassured me they were all okay and had a good laugh about it!

Why would anybody start a bicycle tour somewhere that doesn't have any roads? I had intended to cycle around Venice before setting off on my trip. But obviously hadn't thought it through! There's a clue in the nickname for this place, "city of water!" Just getting from the railway station to a road involved having to carry the bike over a bridge!

Eventually, I found my way to the only road in and out of Venice. It was already busy with busloads of tourists heading to Venice for the day! Just as well, I left!

Bit of a boring ride after leaving Venice, the roads have just been long and straight! I'm hoping the ride will be a bit more exciting tomorrow!

# FRIDAY, 21ST MAY. CASAL BORSITTA TO PESARO. 89 MILES.

Not a good start to the day, I'd been attacked by mosquitoes in the night! And was suffering! I'd also decided to stop taking my pain killers yesterday. I didn't think I needed them anymore as it only hurt when I walked. And as I wasn't walking much, why bother? Boy was I wrong! Bad mistake, an hour into my ride, I was in excruciating pain! And had to stop and take some pain relief! I don't think we'll be trying that one again! After an hour, the pain eased, and I was feeling a lot better. Apart from my mosquitoes bits, they were very annoying, and I couldn't stop itching them!

I passed through Ravenna this morning. As I was cycling towards it, the name rang a bell, but for the life of me, I couldn't think why. Then as I arrived upon Ravenna, it came to me! Chichester, it was twinned with Chichester, somewhere I drive through nearly every day when I'm working! What am I going to think about now that I've worked that one out?

I'm finding the roads hard to navigate! The main road that I would generally have ridden down is more like the M25 but only a single lane! The motorist's give you plenty of room, and I don't feel threatened at all. It's just that it's lorry after lorry, it's been like it since I left Venice 160-miles ago! I tried to take some smaller roads that aren't on my map, but the signs just kept sending me back to the main road! So I've cycled plenty of miles today, but not got very far down the road! I eventually bought another map, it's not much better but, at least it kept me off the main road this afternoon.

## SATURDAY 22ND MAY. PESARO TO SANTA MARIA A MARE. 80 MILES.

Not much to report today, it's been an easy ride with a nice tailwind. The weather's been warm and overcast, ideal cycling weather.

I stopped early today, as I managed to break one of the tent poles when packing away this morning! Luckily I've got a repair kit. So with that and some Gaffer tape, I've managed to repair it. Hopefully, it will last until I get back to the UK.

Expensive campsite tonight and the most I've paid so far, 16 euros!!

# SUNDAY 23ᴿᴰ MAY. SANTA MARIA A MARE TO FOSSACESIA. 84 MILES.

Good news, the pain in my leg seems to have gone. The bad news, I've now got a blister on my bum! As a result, the song that kept going around in my head. Money for nothing, by Dire Straits. And the line that goes "maybe get a blister on your thumb!" Except I replaced the word thumb!

Very hot today, not a cloud in the sky. Pleasant ride, apart from my blister! On my left, there were the tourist beaches with their sunbeds and parasols neatly lined up, in regimental lines! On my right, away in the distance, a range of snow-capped mountains!

I think the winters must be harsh here, there are plenty of road signs with pictures of tyres with snow chains on! Hard to believe in this heat!

Pleasant last 20 miles or so, cycling through small fishing villages, with the fishermen's nets hanging at the end of piers in the beautiful turquoise Adriatic sea.

Fisherman's piers

# MONDAY 23RD MAY. FOSSACESIA TO TRINITAPOLI. 124 MILES.

Long day today! I decided to cut inland and miss out the Gargano peninsular, as it looked a bit mountainous! But then when I'd had enough, I couldn't find a campsite! One of the problems of moving away from the coast. I did consider a spot of wild camping, but couldn't find anywhere suitable! Or maybe I didn't try hard enough, I prefer hotels to wild camping these days!

The last 20-miles of the day were hard going. Apart from the fact that I'd already cycled over 100-miles! I'd now picked up a strong headwind! But finally, I made it to a town that had a hotel. The last few towns had nothing. I knew I should have stopped in Foggia, and I don't know why I didn't. Actually, I do! I did my usual thing, of not deviating of my road, and to just keep going until something turns up! It mostly works, but sometimes it doesn't, and I end up cycling 124-miles!

Never mind, it's all good now, after finding this delightful little hotel in Trinitapoli. It made a pleasant change, to eat my supper on a table, rather than my lap. One of the things that I do miss when camping.

Entertainment today came courtesy of the local prostitutes, and not the way your thinking! They were on the side of the road, every 30 yards or so. So I took it upon myself to get a picture of them, without getting caught, I was worried they may charge me if found out!

I should get to Bari tomorrow, where I could get a ferry to Greece or Turkey. I might take a look overnight, to see if I should change my route!

# TUESDAY 25TH MAY. TRINITAPOLI TO MONOPOLI. 81 MILES.

Obviously, I decided to give Greece and Turkey a miss, I'll save those for future trips!

What a small world we live in. Flicking through the TV last night, I came across Italia's version of "who wants to be a millionaire." Quite entertaining, even though I didn't understand a word they were saying!

Definitely made the right decision, stopping when I did last night. I've only passed 2 campsites all day. Hence, I'm in a hotel again tonight.

The roads have been hard going today, the main highway which, as we all know, would be my favoured route, was classed as a motorway! And closed to bicycles, not that that has stopped me in the past! The minor roads that I've been forced to cycle on leave a lot to be desired! I don't think they've heard of maintenance and filling potholes! It certainly didn't do my blister a lot of good!

I'm going to cut inland again tomorrow, I don't fancy going all the way around the heel of Italy. Hopefully, it won't turn into another long day, as it did on Monday!

# WEDNESDAY 26TH MAY. MONOPOLI TO METAPONTO. 77 MILES.

I've not a good day! Things started to go wrong right from the start! I thought I'd be smart when I left the hotel this morning, I thought I'd be smart! Instead of going back the way I'd come, last night, to get back to the main road, I'd take a shortcut! Some shortcut, what took me 15 minutes yesterday, took over an hour this morning! That set the tone for the day!

Eventually, after finding my way back on to the right road, I then spent the next 4 hours trudging uphill! Then when the tide had turned, and I was heading downhill, I went the wrong way! And had to turn around and head back uphill! It wasn't entirely my fault, the name on the sign that I followed, was very similar to the name of the town I was meant to be heading for!

I think a lot of my problems today, stem from my partaking a little too much in the local vino last night! I knew I shouldn't have had that third carafe! Anyway, I've found a campsite tonight so no vino for Garry, just beer! Hopefully, I'll have a better day tomorrow!

# THURSDAY 27TH MAY. METAPONTO TO ?? NOT TOO SURE. 88 MILES.

Not too sure, where I am tonight but, it's 88 miles further south! I wasn't expecting to stop just yet, but when this campsite popped up, I thought why not! Hence I don't know where I am!

There was a bit of a chill in the air first thing this morning, and it was quite damp. I even had to put my fleece on! But It soon warmed up, and I was back to a t-shirt.

Not much to say today, I've been cycling dual carriageways nearly all day. Looking at the map, I think it may be the same for the next couple of days. There has been a range of mountains to my right, which with there snow-capped peaks, have looked pretty spectacular. And as long as they stay over there, it'll be fine!

Lovely cheap campsite tonight, it's only costing me 5 euros! And I've got the campground to myself. There's nobody else here! After supper, I went to have a look at the sea. But was attacked by something, I haven't got a clue what it was! But it was about the size of a bee, and it made a low buzzing noise, I made a hasty exit and returned to my tent!

## FRIDAY 28TH MAY. NORTH OF CARIATI TO CATANZARO LIDO. 85 MILES.

Still not too sure where I was last night, but the first-named place I came across this morning was Cariati.

It rained in the night, for the first time since I arrived in Italy. It wasn't heavy but did go on for most of the night, and was still raining when I got up at 5 o'clock.

I saw some more prostitutes today, business must have been a bit slow for them, they were all taking pictures of me as I rode past. Perhaps I should have charged them!

I didn't realise that the Mafia known as the "ndrangheta" around these parts, are "allegedly" still around, or so I was reading last night. Which might explain what happened yesterday!

Yesterday I was in a small shop getting my daily supplies and was having a laugh and joke with the lady behind the counter. Not that we understood each other, but I think she was asking me where I was going. "to Sicily, Mafia country" I said. That was it, her smiles and friendly gestures disappeared! And I was quickly served and ushered out of the shop, with the door slamming behind me! At the time, I thought it was a bit odd but never gave it a second thought. But, tonight after reading that the Mafia is "allegedly" still around here. And the reaction I received in the shop, I think they might be!

## SAT 29TH MAY. CANTAZARO LIDO TO BOVA MARINA. 90 MILES.

I had the campsite to myself again last night. With the campsite to myself, I was given the freedom to choose my own pitch. I decided to pitch my tent in a cluster of trees, near the showers, overlooking the sea. I even had a table and chair to sit at. Oh, what heaven to sit on a chair and eat supper at a table, sheer bliss! Strange the things you miss! I sat outside for ages drinking my cans of beer listening to the sea lapping against the shore, I think I even dozed off for a while! Something to do with my age maybe! I enjoyed that campsite.

In stark contrast to tonight's campsite, which I can only describe as a building site! No hot water, trenches everywhere and no electricity anywhere! And they still charged me 15 euros! But as this was the third site, that I'd tried, all the others were closed. So I thought it best to accept what I've got and made the most of it.

Bit of a lonely ride today not much traffic on the roads today, even the towns and villages I passed through, seemed void of all life. The only company I've had is the little green geckos that would scurry away into the undergrowth when I came along.

Lovely scenery today, a bit more what I'd imagined Italy to be like. Very un-touristy.

# SUNDAY 30TH MAY. BOVA MARINA TO ALESSIO SICULO, SICILY. 64 MILES.

Not so many miles today, mainly due to getting lost, a ferry and sightseeing.

I decided last night that I was going to go to Sicily. After all, it's only a ferry ride away. And after a bit of hasty homework last night, I decided to get the ferry from Reggio di Calabria. But when I arrived in Reggio, I got lost and couldn't find the ferry terminal! Oh well, perhaps I won't go to Sicily after all!

I continued to cycle on and reached, Villa San Giovanni, and noticed I could get a ferry from there to Sicily. And I managed to find the terminal this time! When I went to buy a ticket, I got ushered to the boarding area. And before I knew it, I was boarding the ferry! I thought maybe I'd have to pay as I disembarked, but no, I just road off with the other traffic, bargain!

Not too sure if I'm going to cycle all the way around the island yet, I'll see how I get on tomorrow. First impressions though are, that everybody seems very friendly.

Nearly everybody I passed said hello, or should I say "ciao". I Just hope I don't wake up with a horses head next to me tomorrow morning!

Stunning scenery in Sicily

# MONDAY 31ST MAY. ALESSIO SICULO TO CATANIA. 83 MILES.

What a brilliant start to the day, especially as I didn't wake up with a horses head next to me! The ride first thing this morning was stunning! Riding along the SS114 coastal road. On one side, Mount Etna was smouldering away, ominously in the distance! And on the other side the crystal clear waters of Ionian sea.

All was going well, and I was having a good ride until I reached Catania! There I was cycling along quiet happily. When the road I was on turned into a "diversione!"

Keeping an eye on the road signs, so as not to get lost. As I mostly do when it comes to cities, let alone when I'm heading off on some diversion!! I cycled on. It wasn't a pleasant ride, the roads were busy! And to make things worse, I was now going uphill! Then suddenly, without any warning, I'm was on a motorway! What? How did that happen? I did contemplate turning around, but with the amount of traffic coming at me wasn't an option! Well, there wasn't anything I could do about it! The only thing to do was put my head down and pedal like mad! And hope there was an exit soon!

Now over the top of the hill, I was flying along. And was doing about 40mph when a police car came past me, with its light's flashing and siren whaling! That was it I thought I was bound to be stopped, thankfully they carried on! Phew, that was worrying, it certainly made my bum twitch! A few miles further on, I saw the police car in a service area, but no sign of the policemen. I needed to get off this motorway, my nerves couldn't take much more!

Another 5-minutes down the road my luck ran out! And I was pulled over, not by the police, but by highway maintenance, I think? The man was very polite, and in his broken English, he seemed very concerned about my safety. I tried to explain that I was following the diversion, and had ended up on this motorway by mistake! I managed to work out from what he was saying, that there was an exit about 6km away, and I should get off there! Don't worry, I will!

With that, he got back in his car and headed off. I too headed off and yes after about 6km, sure enough, there was an exit! I must admit, riding on a motorway doesn't bother me. After all, I have my own lane, in the hard shoulder. My only worry is being stopped by the police! Off the motorway, I found the road I should have been on.

After a mile or two, I spotted the orange car, with the man in that, had stopped me on the motorway, obviously checking up on me! He needn't have worried, I was glad to be off the motorway! I continued cycling along, thinking that maybe I'll stop soon. I did stop and a lot faster than I thought!

The road had run out! There should have been a bridge here. Instead, there was a fence with a sign on it. The sign read "Ponte chiuso fuori Strada" road closed bridge out! Now I think back, the man who had stopped me on the motorway, kept saying something about a Ponte! Maybe I should have got my phrasebook out! Anyway, there was no way around the fence, and even if there was, the ravine was too deep! Reluctantly I turned around.

Unfortunately, the diversion around the broken bridge was back to the motorway. Not wanting to push my luck back on there, I consulted my map. And the only other way I could see was a massive tour inland! Balls to that, I thought and rode back to Catania. Not via the motorway, I hasten to add.

Back in Catania, I decided to give up on Sicily and head back to the mainland. I had wanted to go back to Villa San Giovanni. But the ferries don't sail there from Catania! Instead, I'm booked on a boat bound for Naples! It seems a bit of a shame to miss out on such a big chunk of Italy, and I could have cycled back to Messina and got the ferry from there. But I didn't fancy cycling back the way I'd already come! So Naples, here we come!

# TUESDAY 1ST JUNE. NAPLES TO GAETA. 70 MILES.

The night crossing from Sicily was okay, and I hunkered down on one of the benches in the ship's café. We arrived in Naples nine hours later, but it took another three hours for the boat to dock, and to be allowed off! I think docking took so long, because of a huge cruise ship, taking up all the room. Once I was off the boat, I wished I'd stayed on it! The roads in Naples are all made of cobbles! After twenty miles of bum numbing cobbles, I was finally out of Naples and on smooth asphalt!

I've found it a hard going today, possibly the lack of sleep last night. And I think those cobbles took a lot out of me! I was glad my blister has nearly gone, although after those cobbles it may be back!

I had a bit of a nightmare trying to find somewhere to stop tonight, the first two campsites that I came across were both closed. And with no campsites insight, I decided it'll have to be a hotel tonight.

The first hotel I came across was down a ridiculously steep road and, had I gone down, I would have never made it back up! The second hotel was also down a steep gradient, but not quite as bad as the first, so I went to enquire about a room for the night. They wanted 100 Euros, a bit expensive but any port in a storm! Unfortunately, they didn't have a restaurant, and there were no other restaurants around either! Also, there was nowhere to leave my bike! I don't think they wanted me to stay! I pushed my bike back up the hill to the main road and continued on my quest to find a bed for the night. In the end, I've found a four-star hotel costing me 130 euros! But at least they have a restaurant, and I've got a bed for the night!

# WEDNESDAY 2ND JUNE. GAETA TO ROME. 100 MILES.

Well, that was an expensive night! 200 euros! And to top it all, an hour down the road this morning I came across a campsite! But that was an hour this morning on fresh legs, and it was already 8 o'clock by the time I'd stopped last night. Although if I'd have spent less time trying other hotels, I might have made it. But to be honest, I had just had enough, I think those cobbles took a lot out of me.

"All roads lead to Rome", or so they say, well they did today! I had a lovely ride into Rome along the tree-lined SS7 via Appia, an old Roman road which used to run all the way to the eastern coast apparently! Rome was lovely as you'd expect, and there were more cobbles, but nowhere as bad as Naples!

Some kind German tourists took my picture in front of the Colosseum. I then decided to leave and find somewhere to stop. That was a nightmare, why do all roads in and out of cities, turn into motorways! I know they don't, but on my maps they do! Pulling away from some traffic lights, I managed to snap a toe-clip off one of my pedals! That was the fault of the cobbles, or that's what I'm blaming! In a rush to pull away from the lights, I went to put my foot into the toe-clip. At the same time, I hit a large cobble. And instead of putting my foot in the clip. My foot landed on top of it and snapped it off! I stopped to retrieve it, in the hope that maybe I'll be able to fix it at some point. Not today, though, I was too tired!

Eventually, I found my way out of Rome and even managed to find a campsite. Although it's a bit expensive at 25 euros, but compared to last nights hotel, it's a bargain! It does seem to be costly along this coast, but I suppose it's because there are so many tourists about!

It just had to be done

# THURSDAY 3RD JUNE. 12 MILES OUT OF ROME TO ALBINIA. 96 MILES.

Before leaving the campsite this morning, I repaired my broken toe-clip, with the help of cable ties. I've always said you can fix anything with gaffer tape and cable ties!

I forgot to mention yesterday, but I had a bit of scare when I managed to end up on another motorway! I miss read the signs, once again! As I mentioned before, being on the highway isn't that bad as I'm in my own lane, on the hard shoulder. But this time it ran out when I had to go through a tunnel! I was kicking myself, how did I manage to end up here! But there was nothing I could do about it now. I just needed to get through this 3km tunnel! To say I was scared was a bit of an understatement, I was crapping myself! Lorries were speeding past within inches of me! Even though I was riding as close to the curb as I could! Riding that close made it hard to avoid the drains, which are never level with the road! Some of them were so deep, I thought my wheels were going to collapse, or I was going to come off! It was a long 3km, and I was glad to make it out of the tunnel, alive!

A pretty none eventful ride today, but I did notice how the landscape has changed. I've gone from fields of grapevines to fields of wheat and barley. And if it wasn't for the odd cactus here and there, I could be at home in England. I also got caught in a thunderstorm at the end of the day!

# FRIDAY 4TH JUNE. ALBINIA.

I decided to take the day off today, my first in three weeks. I'm on a lovely campsite that has everything I want and need! They have a supermarket, clean hot showers, a launderette, so I can give my clothes a proper wash. It's not quite the same washing them in the shower. Even if it is every day! It's cheap, compared with what I've been paying, at 11 euros a night! And most importantly they have an excellent little bar!

The other reason for staying put today, I've got a couple of weeks work in Samoens, France. But if my leg is still bad and I can't weight bear on it, I won't bother. And after spending the last few weeks just sitting on my bike, I really need to know how good I am, at standing for any time!

After washing all my clothes and sleeping bag in the launderette first thing this morning, I hope my sleeping bag dry's in time for tonight! I sat around in my swimming shorts, waiting for something to dry! In the end, I gave up and put my clothes on wet and cycled into town. It's so warm they soon dried. In town, I decided to go for a haircut and shave, and if any bodies in Albinia I can recommend a good barber, Paulo Conti!

Not a lot to Albinia, just a few shops and a couple of cafés. After having lunch, I headed back to camp. On the way back, I stopped to look at the beach, but there wasn't a lot going on there! Back at camp, my sleeping bag was nearly dry. Which was a relief I didn't fancy sleeping in a wet bag! After walking around the campsite a few times, checking my leg out, I headed for the bar!

# SATURDAY 5TH JUNE. ALBINIA TO MARINA DI CASTAGNETO DONORATICO. 86 MILES.

Haha, I had an amusing night in the bar last night watching the children's entertainment! The entertainer didn't look much older than her audience! Maybe that's a sign of me getting old! She was good though, and I think I enjoyed it more than the children! Not too sure what time I got back to my tent, but it was late, and was a bit worse for wear!

I had to buy a new front tyre today after the old one had worn out and was down to the webbing! I only noticed it while sitting on a bench having a break. Worryingly though, I had just flown down a hill, and reached 52mph! If it had blown on me then, well it's not worth thinking about! Thankfully there are plenty of bicycle shops around. Unfortunately, they are more geared up to the lycra brigade, and I couldn't find a tyre of the right width! 26 by 175 tyres seems to be hard to get. Funnily enough, I had the same problem in Portugal last year! The new tyre is 26 by 150, so there's not too much difference, and I'm sure it will be fine.

I met two fellow British cycle tourists from Gloucester Phil and Phil! This morning. They'd flown into Genoa, and cycled down to Sicily. They were now on there way back to Genoa to catch their flight home. It was nice to have a conversation with somebody in English and not broken English! In fact, they're the first English people I've met and had a conversation with since leaving the UK! Apart from two women that I'd spoken to very briefly, in Naples, they were on the cruise around the med and were just in Naples for the day.

The two Phils

# SUNDAY 6TH JUNE. MARINA DI CASTA TO MARINA DI CARRARA. 80 MILES.

I've had a good ride today on quiet roads. Much of it has been spent cycling along the service roads, running parallel with the autostrada. They were excellent, and I stopped at one of the motorway services for an ice cream! Some of the looks I got from cars pulling off the autostrada, with me sat there, bike fully loaded eating an ice cream! I think they all thought that I had cycled up the motorway to get there!

I cycled through Pisa today, and of course, diverted to see the tower. The Piazza di Miracol where the famous leaning tower of Pisa is located, along with the Grand Cathedral and Baptistry were stunning! And looked magnificent along with the immaculate green lawns of the Piazza. That tower leans at quite an angle! Surprisingly it wasn't that busy, or maybe the main body of tourists hadn't arrived yet!

Now, what was I saying about not meeting anybody from England? And although there weren't that many people in the Piazza. The ones that were there were all seemed to be English! It was nice to talk to them, even if they did all asked the same questions; where have you cycled from? Where are you cycling? It's always nice when people ask about what I'm doing, and most people are impressed!

I passed the 10,000-mile mark today, not on this trip, but since I bought the bike two years ago! Not bad going really, considering three years ago the furthest I'd ever cycled was probably about ten miles! Today is also the first day since leaving home that I haven't taken any painkillers! Things are looking up, I might have to have a beer or two to celebrate tonight!

Piazza di Miracol

# MONDAY 7TH JUNE. MARINA DI CARRARA TO RAPALLO. 72 MILES.

A fresh, overcast day today, which as it turned out, was ideal for the ride ahead! I've had some rather hard hills to get up today, with the hardest being the "Passo del Bracco" at 615 metres!! It was a long winding road, up through pine forests. As I climbed higher, I looked down and could see the autostrada disappearing in and out of tunnels. Carving the flattest route through the mountains. Every time I turned a corner, I thought I would be at the top, not a chance, this hill just continued up! I thought I was going to need oxygen if I kept going any higher! Slight exaggeration, I know, but you get my drift.

Once at the top, coming down the other side was great fun, albeit a bit chilly. The road going down was more twisting and turning than the route up! I don't think it was really, it was just that I was going faster! I'd fly along for two or three hundred yards, trying to beat the 52mph I'd achieved earlier on in the tour. Before I'd have to slam on my brakes to get around the hairpin bend. I was causing a bit of a tailback, with cars unable to overtake me. I think they were a bit surprised at my turn of speed along the straight! Although I did slow down frequently to let them pass. Looking at my map, I think it might be like this all the way to France! That'll be fun!

# TUESDAY 8TH JUNE. RAPALLO TO ALBENGA. 80 MILES.

I made sure I had plenty of pasta to eat last night, as I was expecting another hard ride today! I wasn't disappointed! More long slow climbs followed by fast downhill rides! I passed through Genoa today and wondered if the two Phil's from Gloucester, that I had met a few days ago had made it. I think their flight home was today.

Cycling through Genoa was hard work! And for once, it wasn't my inability to find my way, the roads were pretty straight forward. It was the traffic, it was so busy! And as for the pollution, it was chocking! Getting through seemed to take forever. After eventually making it through Genoa, I found myself on the outskirts, in an industrial area. When all of a sudden, a deer ran across the road! Poor thing must have been petrified, it was well out of its usual surroundings! And as to how it got there?

Out of Genoa, the ride was absolutely stunning! Near on vertical hills, plunging down to the sea, with palm trees on their slopes and houses clinging precariously to the rocks. Looking as if they were going to topple into the sea at any moment! Every town I rode through today, after Genoa, had streets lined with palm trees. Which, in one village, caused a bit of a hold-up. One of them had fallen over, closing the road. Once the road had been cleared, I was the first through, which on the narrow road wasn't great! Especially when there was a great big artic, hot on my heels! I soon pulled over and let him pass, along with the thirty or forty other vehicles!

# WEDNESDAY 9TH JUNE. ALBENGA TO MENTON, FRANCE. 75 MILES.

Some squawking seagulls kept me awake for the best part of the night last night! Leaving me feeling pretty tired this morning! And although I don't tend to need a lot of sleep. What sleep I do have is generally deep, and I didn't get much of either last night!

I should have started to head inland today. Instead, I crossed the border into France and headed to Monaco! It seemed to be a bit stupid not to go, seeing as I was so close. As I rode to Monaco, the yachts in the marina's seemed to get bigger and more expensive the closer I got to Monaco! Every town I passed through had a marina and the ones that didn't were busy building one!

I got to Monaco and looked a bit out of place amongst all the glitz and glamour! Or what some peoples perception of glamour is! I was too late for the Grand Prix race, although there were still some remnants of it. Only some scaffolding, from one of the stands. But on the road, there was still plenty of rubber laid down by the cars! Being a bit of an F1 fan, I decided to ride the circuit. And managed to ride it in about 13 minutes 22 seconds! Not quite as fast as a Formula 1 car, but then they don't have the traffic to contend with! And an F1 car probably weighs less than what I carry!

After pratting around in Monaco for a couple of hours, I headed back on myself to Menton. I decided the other day that my leg was feeling okay and I would go to Samoens. I've also been off the painkillers for a few days, and still, feel fine. Despite having some pretty hard cycling!

Casino Square Monaco

# THURSDAY 10TH JUNE. MENTON TO SAVIGIANO. 81 MILES.

Another tough ride today, and it took me nearly eight hours to cycle 17-miles this morning! After looking at the map last night. I decided that my best route to Samoens was via Turin, Aosta and Chamonix. But to do this, I had to cycle back to Italy, something I hate!

After returning to Italy, I headed up the SS20, which ran beside the river Roya. The SS20 was on a gentle gradient, with the river Roya on one side, and a railway line on the other. Cycling along, I looked at my map, there was a 1279-metre pass ahead! I hadn't seen that last night, or maybe I chose not to see it! There was nothing I could do about now, I certainly wasn't going to turn around! And to be honest, if the road stays at this gradient, it'll be fine.

It was pretty fantastic riding up through the gorges, with their sheer rock faces. With just the road and the river between them! As I rode up, I would come across hydro stations making use of the mountain water, and villages perched high up on the mountainsides. After a few hours of cycling, I came across a little shop and thought I'd stop to get something to eat. There wasn't a lot in there, just some soap, razor blades and various other random items that were of no use to me at all! But on the counter, they had some cold pizza and a couple of small cans of coke. I bought them all! The pizza was divine and hit the right spot!

Another couple of hours passed of this uphill cycle, and I was starting to feel tired! Then turning a corner, I saw the snow-capped peak of Col de Tende. And thought, there can't be much further to go. With renewed vigour, I speeded up! Only to be thwarted a short distance up the road, with a sign saying 15Km to go! I'd been going for hours, and I'd only come 10km! The last 5km was really hard, with the road turning into a 14% gradient!

Finally! I reached the top. To be greeted with a tunnel, saying no bicycles! What? Balls to that, I'd spent 8 hours getting up here, and if you think I'm going back you can think again! So with a final burst of energy, I started the 3km ride through the tunnel! Every 200 hundred metres or so, markers were pointing the way to the emergency exit. Every time one would pop up I'd think, a quarter of the way through, halfway through! Three-quarters of a way through! Surely if I get stopped now, they'll let me continue! Finally, I was through the tunnel and hadn't been caught. Once through the tunnel, I hurridly put a couple of extra layers on ready for the downhill. I didn't want to hang around just in case somebody did challenge me as to how I got there!

After the tunnel, I made good speed, as you would expect and cycled the remaining 64-miles of my day in four hours. Unable to find a campsite tonight, I'm staying in a hotel.

The river Roya, looking more like a stream now

# FRIDAY 11TH JUNE. SAVIGLIANO TO IVREA. 81 MILES.

Nasty experience in the hotel restaurant last night, after swallowing a piece of meat that was too big! And getting it stuck in my throat! And I do mean stuck! Nothing I tried would dislodge it. Coughing, or swallowing, didn't have any effect! Taking a sip of wine, hoping that, may do the trick, didn't help either! It just sat on top of the meat swishing around in my throat! I wondered if I could get somebody to perform the Heimlich manoeuvre on me!

But I was sat in a restaurant in a foreign country, with nobody speaking my language or me there's! How will they know what's wrong with me? I was close to panicking, as I could feel my chest tightening, through lack of air!  But, with one final cough and a splutter, it flew out of my mouth and across the table! Along with the red wine, making quite a mess on the crisp white table cloth! Thank god for that, I wasn't going to die in some foreign country after all! It was quite a frightening experience! Something I've never had before, and something I don't particularly want to have it ever again.

Easy ride today, compared to yesterday, it's been pretty flat. Apart from the last 12-miles or so. But then I am heading towards the Alps! Tomorrow is going to be a tough day! I passed through Turin today and had more cobbled streets, thankfully it wasn't as bad as Naples! I should make it to Aosta tomorrow. I'll then decide if I'm going to tackle the Col du Grand St-Bernard at 2473-metres! Or take the easy option and get the bus through the Monte Blanc tunnel!

## SATURDAY 12TH JUNE. IVREA TO CHAMONIX. 52 MILES.

I had a short ride up the picturesque Valle D'Aosta this morning, surrounded by high mountains. Unfortunately, the clouds were too low, for me to see the tops. But every so often the clouds would lift, and reveal their high peaks, shining brightly in the sun! I kept looking at the mountains towering high above me, as I cycled towards Aosta. And in the end, I decided I didn't want to cycle over them, I'd prefer to just look at them from down here!! And opted to ride up to Courmayeur and go through the Mont Blanc Tunnel.

It was a bit of a panic when I arrived at Courmayeur. The last bus of the day was about to leave! And there wasn't another one until Monday! I removed my panniers as quickly as possible. And put them along with my bike, in the belly of the bus! As the driver hovered impatiently over me, waiting for me to finish! Thankfully a couple of American hikers took pity on me and helped me lift the bike in.

The bus ride through the tunnel isn't cheap at 18 euros, and it wasn't as expected! I was expecting a bright modern, concrete-lined tunnel, similar to the ones I'd already cycled through. Instead, the tunnel was narrow and dark, with jagged granite walls. The only light was the light from the headlights of the cars coming in the opposite direction! But at least it saved me from cycling over the 2473 metres of the Col du Grand St-Bernard!

After arriving in Chamonix, I put my bike back together and went to the nearest campsite. Which is apparently beneath Mont Blanc, I can't tell, the cloud bass is too low. Hopefully, the clouds will lift tomorrow, and I'll get a glimpse. Just off to the bar with the two American hikers, who helped me in Courmayeur. We're off to watch England's opening game to the world cup, ironically we're playing the USA!

# SUNDAY 13<sup>TH</sup> JUNE. CHAMONIX TO SAMOENS. 47 MILES.

It was good to see England get off to their usual rubbish start, let's hope they improve! But in the interest of fairness, it was probably fitting that we drew with the USA, considering I was watching it with a couple of Americans!

Up at the crack of dawn, as per normal. I wanted to be on the road nice and early, and get to Samoens as early as possible. So I could suss out what I needed to do. As I crawled out of the tent, I looked up to see if I could see Mont Blanc. Not a chance the cloud base was even lower today! I had breakfast, and kept looking up at the mountain, in the hope, that the clouds had lifted, not a chance!

I packed away and started to leave camp, just as the clouds began to lift! Wow, what a sight, we don't get mountains of this magnitude in the UK! They do fascinate me, as long as I'm not cycling over them!

What a great start to my ride, seeing Mont Blanc, emerge from the clouds! It took me ages to get out of Chamonix. I kept stopping to look and take photos, as the clouds would come and go, revealing different vistas. As I cycled down the valley, away from Chamonix, I turned around to take one last look. But the clouds had descended, and the mountain had once again disappeared behind a blanket of clouds.

The ride to Samoens was non-eventful. And let's face it after seeing Mont Blanc, it would have, had to have been something pretty spectacular to beat that! I'm now at a campsite in Samoens, where all being well and good with my leg, I shall remain for a couple of weeks. I should have been staying in the chalet, I'm working on. But after spotting the campsite in Samoens, I decided to camp. Even if I'll have a 115-metre, one-mile climb each morning to get to work!

# SATURDAY 3^{RD} JULY. SAMOENS TO NANTUA. 77 MILES.

Well, it's been three weeks, but finally, I'm on the move! There was a little more work than I thought. Definitely a good move camping, despite the tough ride up the hill every morning! But, at the end of the day, what a blast flying down the mountain! Something that has taken me a bit of getting used to shadows! The shadows from the mountains. The chalet was only in sunlight for part of the day. The day would start with the chalet in full sunlight, but as the sun rose and moved across the sky, we would be cast into the shadow of the mountain! It's just something we don't get back home!

It's been a busy three weeks, and I've been out of contact with everybody! The only internet café in Samoens wasn't open in the evenings! And I've only taken two days off, in the past three weeks. One of my days off was a jolly to Chamonix. I wanted to see Mont Blanc again and ride the cable car up to the Aiguille du Midi, the closest I was going to get, to going up Mont Blanc! I caught the 8.15 bus from Samoens and arrived in Chamonix an hour and forty minutes later. It was still early, and there was only a short queue to ride the cable car.

Once on the cable car, they crammed us in like sardines, to get as many people in as possible! A coach load of American tourists had just pulled up, and it had suddenly become busy! The ride up in the cable car was like a roller coaster ride! Each time we went over a pylon, the car dropped, leaving my stomach in the air!

At the top, the views were breathtaking! Chamonix far below looked so small! I was glad to have a clear day and could see for miles. While up there, I took the cable car across to the Italian border. A scenic ride across glaciers and snow plains, down below I could see lines of climbers setting out across the vast whiteness of snow. In the distance, there was a range of jagged mountain peaks, waiting to be climbed, by those that were brave enough! It was an enjoyable day!

But now I'm back on the road heading home, via Switzerland, I need to go to the bank! A very brief visit and I only cycled about 20-miles on Swiss soil! But it'll be another country to add to the countries I've cycled on this tour! I've found cycling today tough going! It was okay on the way to Switzerland. But after leaving Geneva, I found it hard! It may have been because it was hot, temperatures were in the 30's! Or maybe it's because I've only cycled 83-miles in the past three weeks! Although they have been a tough 83-miles, and I've worked out that I'd climbed 2,185 metres going uphill each day to work!

I hadn't realised, until today that Switzerland has still got its own currency. I thought they had the euro, the same as the countries around it! And it only dawned on me when I went to buy a drink. Thankfully I realised before actually trying to buy it! Don't want to look like an idiot, do we! Well, no more than usual!

Climbers heading out into the mountains

The view from the cable car to Italy

# SUNDAY 4<sup>TH</sup> JULY. NANTUA TO CHAROLLES. 89 MILES.

Not a particularly good nights sleep last night, I was kept awake for much of it by a storm. I could hear the thunder rumbling away in the distance, from early evening, as I ate my supper. And every now and then I would catch sight of a fork of lightening reaching down from the sky. The storm was still rumbling away when I turned in for the night at around 11pm.

As I started to fall asleep, the wind picked up, and the storm was getting louder! As a precaution, I got up and put the guy ropes out. Yes, I know you're always meant to put them out, but who does? Just as well, I did! When the storm hit, it was rather violent, strong winds, heavy rain, thunder! And lightning that would light the tent up, as if it was daylight! The storm seemed to last for a couple of hours, and as it drifted off into the distance, I too drifted off, to sleep! But not for long, although the storm had passed, it started to rain, which, in a tent, is always loud! And before I knew where I was my alarm was going off and it was time to get up!

Tough going this morning, possibly due to the lack of sleep, but then it was hill after hill! I even stopped in Macon and had a little nap on one of the benches! Which seemed to help, but I've still struggled this afternoon, and I never stopped cycling until 7pm!

# SUNDAY 5TH JULY CHAROLLES TO NEVERS. 90 MILES.

As I was feeling tired last night, I went out to the local restaurant for something to eat. It was hard work! I didn't understand the menu, I didn't understand the staff and the staff didn't understand me! Although it was quite amusing ordering something from the menu, not knowing what I was getting! Then the wine menu came out, no beer in here, it was too posh! I ordered a bottle of red, no point in just ordering a glass! Luckily I chose right as the meal I had was lamb, I think! Fortunately, I'm not going to have that problem tonight, as I'm not dining alone!

I'd only been cycling for a short time this morning. When I picked up a pleasant cycle route running beside a canal. I wasn't too sure where it was going, but I was enjoying it so much I stuck with it! It did seem to be heading in the general direction I wanted to go! After an hour of cycling next to the canal, I arrived in Digoin, and thought it might be a good idea to look at the map! As I stood there on a viaduct, looking at my map, a fellow cycle tourist came along. Always keen to talk to other cyclists, I started with my usual line!

"Hi, do you speak English?"

"Yes" came the reply, in almost perfect English. The fellow cyclist was an attractive female!

"do you know where this canal goes to?" I asked

"it's part of Eurovelo route 6, which goes to Nantes" she replied, "I'm cycling it."

Hmm, I could cycle to Nantes, then follow the coast back up to the ferries. I certainly wouldn't mind cycling with you! I thought to myself! Behave yourself, Garry, stick to your own route, but I don't have a route! We continued to talk for a while, and I learnt that she had spent the night in Digoin. She was from Switzerland and had started her ride from lake Constance in Switzerland. She spoke excellent English. In the end, I thanked her for her help and wished her well on her trip. And with that, left her taking pictures while I cycled across the viaduct.

I was annoyed with myself for leaving and wished I'd stayed talking to her, but it was too late I was halfway across the viaduct! I reached the other side of the bridge and stopped to take some photos, well that was my excuse! It worked, Katrin, as I later found out. Came across the bridge, and we started talking once more. After that, we started to cycle together!

We'd been cycling together for a good couple of hours, merrily chatting away when we came to a big hill! We'd already been up, and down a few hills, and Katrin was strong on the hills, often leaving me behind! She's from Switzerland and used to mountains, I was also carrying a lot more weight! This was a big hill, and I didn't want to hold Katrin back. So reluctantly I told her to go on and leave me behind! I said that I had enjoyed our ride together and wished her well on her trip, once again! And with that, I saw her gradually pull away from me. Until she finally disappeared around a bend. I hoped that I might see her again once I had reached the corner, but she was nowhere to be seen! I felt pretty sad at that moment, but there was nothing I could do about it!

Finally, I reached the top of the hill and turning the corner to a shop, there was Katrin! Who had stopped at the shop! I can't explain what a joy it was to see her. Nervously I asked if she was about to leave, secretly hoping that she wasn't! If not could she watch my bike while I went in the shop? Of course, she said. And with that, we were back together!

We spent the rest of the day cycling together, I didn't know where I was going I was just following Katrin! We stopped for a coffee in Dezice, something I never normally do. I'm quite happy to just get a bottle of coke from a shop and find a bench or something to sit on! This was a new experience for me, but being with somebody, it was okay and quite enjoyable.

We arrived in Nevers, and I decided to stay at the same hotel as Katrin. Another new experience for me, Katrin went to the local tourist office to find a hotel! I usually just turn up a hotel desk and ask if they have a room! But then, I suppose if you speak French as well as Katrin, yes she spoke French, as well as English, and

German too! I waited outside while Katrin sorted out a couple of rooms for us. This was easy, I'm enjoying this, having somebody to sort my accommodation out!

It's been a fantastic day, cycling along with Katrin! I'm not usually very good at cycling with somebody else, but for some reason today has been a joy! I'll now be following the Loire Valley for a few days, with Katrin!

The bridge at Digoin

# TUESDAY 6<sup>TH</sup> JULY NEVERS TO GIEN. 82 MILES.

Last night in Nevers Katrin and I went out for a delightful meal in a restaurant near to the "Palace of Nevers." Katrin tried to match me, beer for beer, unfortunately, she doesn't know me! And she ended up a little tipsy! There must have been a wedding or something going on. There was a parade of cars, driving around and around tooting their horns. After supper, we went for a little walk around Never's before returning to the hotel.

It's been a lovely flat ride today, following the cycle paths along the Loire. Made all the better, by cycling with Katrin. Unfortunately, Katrin has to return to Switzerland in a few days. Which isn't enough time for us to both cycle Loire Valley, but I might continue on my own, I'm enjoying it so much!

We arrived in Gien and headed straight for the "Office de Tourisme", and my tour planner went inside to book a couple of rooms! I like the look on the officers face when Katrin asks for two rooms! But then I don't know if that's what Katrin is asking! Katrin managed to book us into a hotel on the other side of the Loire. I must say, the two hotels that I've stopped at with Katrin have been outstanding when it comes to the bikes. Both have had dedicated garages to store them in!

After checking into our hotel and showering, I went down to the hotel bar and waited for Katrin. I rushed my shower, just to make sure I could get a beer before we went out exploring! And to write my daily blog, I always find it easier with a beer in my hand! Katrin has just arrived, so we're off to explore Gien.

# WEDNESDAY 7TH JULY. GIEN TO ORLEANS. 56 MILES.

Not a good start to the day! I was woken at 3am by a rumbling in my tummy! Not the I'm hungry rumble, that horrible feeling that you need to get to the bathroom asap! I then spent, what was left of the night in and out of the toilet! So glad I was staying in a hotel! I knew that seafood platter last night was a mistake! I blame Katrin, she told me to have it!

Last night after exploring Gien, and eating supper, oh yes the seafood platter! We walked back across the bridge to our hotel. It was dark now, and all that could be heard as we crossed the bridge was a chorus of frogs croaking in the night. It felt quite special!

Because of my stomach, I didn't have too much to eat at breakfast. Just coffee, toast and some Imodium! After breakfast, we retrieved our bikes from the garage and set off along the Loire once more. Katrin did ask me if I was okay to ride. I would have said yes whether I was or not!

Another nice ride today, although we did pick up another cyclist that wanted to join us! Cycling along, we came across a cyclist by the side of the track. So we stopped to make sure he was okay, but he didn't speak English. Not a problem, I have my own translator! Although Katrin did say later that she struggled to understand him, with his strong accent. It turned out that he was fine, so we continued on our way.

A few minutes later, he was behind us asking us where we were going, and which way we were going to go. Or so my translator told me! He kept talking, and Katrin kept translating for me. He was a bit persistent and wouldn't stop talking. In the end, we dropped back a bit, and when we came to a fork in the road, we made sure we took the opposite one to him. Regardless of whether or not it was the way we wanted to go! We spent the next hour looking over our shoulders, but we never saw him again.

We came across an impressive Chateau after we'd managed to lose our tag! Chateaux Sully-sur-Loire, an imposing fortress, with its thick-set walls and fairy tale towers surrounded by a wide moat. We took a few photos there!

What was I saying yesterday about hotels, having parking areas for bikes? I take it back! Tonight's hotel didn't have a garage, but they did let us leave them in the corridor. The only problem, the corridor was up a narrow flight of stairs, as was the hotel!

We're going to be staying in Orleans for two nights, as it's an easy place for Katrin to get the train to Paris on Friday. I think tomorrow we're going to really play the tourist and visit a Chateau!

Chateaux Sully-sur-Loire

# THURSDAY 8TH JULY. ORLEANS TO BLOIS. 52 MILES.

We found another pleasant restaurant last night "Le Petite Marmite" set in an old timber-framed house. And despite having a bad stomach, earlier on in the day. I went for the snails, I had wanted frogs legs, but I think they're out of season! As we sat in the restaurant, we got talking another couple, who were also dining there. We had a pleasant chat with them, and they couldn't believe that we were not a couple. And had only just met! They said that we made a lovely couple and that things would change! We both blushed and laughed it off! Neither of us was looking for love! We were just enjoying ourselves, as friends.

Breakfast was a little basic this morning! I was very disappointed, especially as I had missed out on a lovely breakfast at yesterday's hotel! After breakfast, I carried the bikes down the stairs of the hotel. Which was a lot easier this morning without any luggage on them. Once out of the hotel, we set off for Chateau de Chambord.

The ride to Chambord took us through fields of sunflowers, with their bright yellow heads. And fields of grapevines, in their near-perfect straight lines. It was easy riding without the burden of panniers, although it did feel a little strange! I'm so used to cycling with a fully loaded bike, especially as I've now cycled nearly 3000 miles on this trip! As we cycled along, we came across swarms of little flies, which is fine if you spot them. But if you don't and your talking, it isn't very nice! Still, on a bright note, I've had my daily quota of protein! Apparently, it's a sign of rain, so Katrin said! And I must admit it did rain later!

We arrived at the Chateau and done the tourist bit. Not really my cup of tea, but I did enjoy parts of it, like the double-helix staircase, and the rooftop terrace. I was doing it more because Katrin wanted to do it, and obviously, I wanted to be with her! After the Chateau we took a short ride to Blois. There we wandered around the steep, narrow streets, of the old city. Which was up a flight of stairs, there must have been over a hundred steps! At the top, I thought to myself, I wouldn't have been able to do that at the beginning of this tour, not even half of them!

After a late lunch and a few beers, we caught the train back to Orleans. On the train, I was starting to feel sad. Thinking that this would be my last day with Katrin. And tomorrow I would be back to cycling alone! That was it! I decided I wasn't going to continue along the Loire Valley alone, it just wouldn't be the same! I decided that I too was going to catch the train to Paris, as long as Katrin didn't mind! And cycle home from there! I mentioned my plan to her, and she seemed happy, but sad at the same time. Perhaps she felt the same way as me!

We returned to the same restaurant in the evening, but there was an air of sadness hanging over the pair of us! I don't think that either of us wanted this tour to stop, I know I certainly didn't! But Katrin had booked her train home, and that was that!

Garry and Katrin on the roof of Chambord

# FRIDAY 9TH JULY. ORLEANS TO PARIS BY TRAIN THEN CYCLE TO CERGY. 39 MILES.

A sad day today, it was my last day with Katrin! As we sat in the small breakfast room, this morning, there was a hushed silence! Usually, we were full of chat, planning our day ahead, not today! And you would have had a job to stop us talking, but now at our last breakfast, we both sat in an eerie silence! We paid our bills at the hotel and took the short ride across the road to the railway station.

The train pulled into the station, and I loaded the bikes on, while Katrin found us a carriage. As the train pulled out of the station, there was a deep sadness that descended upon me! This was it, the final leg, this time tomorrow I would be all alone! I could sense that Katrin was just as sad as I was, as she cuddled up to me, with tears in her eyes, as there was mine! We stayed that way all the way to Paris, making the most of our last few hours together! Maybe I should have made a move earlier! But that wouldn't have been fair to Katrin, she had a boyfriend back home in Switzerland.

We hardly talked, all the way to Paris, we were just enjoying being close, the closest we'd been on our journey! Perhaps we had both been suppressing our feelings! One thing that we did talk about though. That someday we would continue our ride together, along the Loire Valley! And as lovely, a thought as that was, I wasn't convinced that it would ever happen! That was in the future, it didn't help the way I was feeling at the moment! I didn't want Katrin to leave! Arriving in Paris and pulled ourselves together, determined to make the most of our last few hours together.

We cycled around Paris, getting our photos taken with all the major sights! We then went for one last coffee together! Before to Gare de Lyon, to see Katrin off! We arrived early, before the train was there, which didn't help, it just prolonged the agony of saying goodbye!

This was it, we really were at the end of our tour. I watched as Katrin loaded her bike onto the TGV, thinking that, that was my job earlier today! But no longer, we were parting and going our separate ways! Katrin had a bit of trouble getting her bike on the train. After somebody else had taken her space! Katrin soon sorted it out though, and came back off the train, for our final goodbye! I wished I was taking the train with her!

We hugged, said our final goodbye's and vowed that we would meet up again! Neither of us wanted to part, but the train was due to depart. I let Katrin go and said I'm not going to watch the train depart! I couldn't, I could feel the tears welling up inside me, I'd not felt this sad in a long time! And with that, I wheeled my bike off the platform, as the train pulled slowly out of the station!

Outside the station, it was time for me to head home alone! But my heart just wasn't in it! I hadn't wanted it to end this way! I didn't know what way I had wanted it to end, I just didn't! Maybe I'll feel better once I start cycling.

I never did feel better and was just cycling along with no direction or purpose. Eventually, though I found my way to Cergy and checked into a business type hotel. In the hope that they would have a computer, I wanted to check my email just in

case Katrin had e1
about me already!

Garry and Katrin in Paris

# SATURDAY 10TH JULY. CERGY TO ROUEN. 84 MILES.

Right, let's get going! Katrin has gone, back to her life in Switzerland, and isn't going to bother with me! It was just one of those holiday romance things! Well, that's what I told myself as I left the hotel this morning. But inside I hoped it wasn't and longed to be back with Katrin!

My heart wasn't in this tour anymore, it just wasn't the same! And I wanted it to end! I ended up in a quarry, thinking I was following a cycle route! But I didn't care! My enthusiasm and drive had gone!

Eventually, I found my way out of the quarry, but I wouldn't have worried if I didn't, what was the point in carrying on! Everything was a struggle, the wind was against me. Little midges were annoying me and even the slightest hill, felt like a mountain! I was glad to finish!

I'm staying in another business hotel tonight. I wanted to check my emails! Just in case Katrin had written to me! And I'm paying for that privilege! They charged me a fortune for my room. They even charged me to park my bike in the underground car park! But it's worth it if I can check my emails. After showering, I went down to reception to use the public computer. I was apprehensive and excited about checking my emails! Please let there be an email from Katrin! There wasn't, and needless to say, my heart sank once more!

I retired to the bar to write my daily blog. It should have been a happy evening, I'd passed the 3000-mile mark today! Something I'd wanted to achieve at the beginning of this trip. But now it didn't seem to matter, I was pining for Katrin too much! As I sat at the bar, I got latched onto by some self-opinionated boring bloke from North Wales! God, he was annoying! Usually, I'm happy to talk to anybody. But not tonight. Tonight I just wanted to be on my own! I got up, making the excuse that I was going to the toilet, and just walked out of the hotel! Leaving Mr Boring alone, I even left my pint behind! I just wanted to be on my own.

# SUNDAY 11TH JULY. ROUEN TO BOGNOR REGIS. 84 MILES.

I'd found a lovely little Afghanistan restaurant, after walking out the hotel last night. Mr Boring had done me a favour! Had he not come along I would have probably just eaten in the expensive hotel restaurant! I saw him briefly at breakfast this morning, but he was too busy boring somebody else to see me!

There wasn't any rush today, I only had about 50-miles to cycle to Le Havre, and my ferry wasn't due to leave until this evening. I was still on the road early, as I said yesterday, I just want this tour to end!

As I cycled along, I started to reflect on this tour. From being shouted at in Holland, for cycling on the road! Getting on the wrong half of the train in Munich! Finding the bridge had gone in Sicily. Those awful cobbles in Naples, the glamour and glitz of Monaco. And of course, meeting Katrin. That was the highlight of my tour! Spending the day cycling along the picturesque Loire. Stopping for coffee breaks! Staying in hotels, exploring the streets and alleyways of the towns we stopped in. Sharing a meal with at the end of the day. And generally having somebody, to share the experience with. No, not somebody! Katrin, it was good to share the experience with her! All in all, it's been an excellent tour, even though I'm feeling rather low at the moment!

I then started to think of where I should cycle to on my next tour when my phone rang! Who was that? Bloody sales call no doubt! I'm just in the mood for them! But It wasn't a sales call, it was Katrin!

My mood lifted immediately, and I had a broad smile on my face! I couldn't believe she was ringing me! I answered as quickly as possible, I didn't want to miss her call! Unfortunately, I wasn't on a good stretch of road to stop and talk! After answering the phone and saying hello, It was lovely to hear her voice. Could I call you back, in a minute or two I asked when I'm somewhere better? Of course, she said.

I raced along the road to reach a quiet spot, so I could sit and talk to Katrin. Luckily I came across a bus stop, which conveniently had a bus shelter with a bench in it!

I sat on the bench, talking to Katrin for ages, about all sorts of things, but the most exciting news! Katrin had sorted out things out at home. And can return to the Loire Valley next week, that is if I wasn't busy! Busy? Not a chance! If she said, she was on her way there now. I would have turned around there and then! To think, this time next week I would be heading back to the Loire Valley to meet Katrin! My mood changed almost instantly!

I couldn't believe how much my spirits had lifted! The rest of my ride to Le Havre was a breeze, I'd got my mojo back!

The ferry back to England passed quickly, with people asking about my trip. I just wanted to talk about my next trip! Back to the Loire Valley and back to Katrin!

I walked through my front door at 11pm after cycling 3095 miles.

I've just got time to wash my clothes before I head back to France!

Printed in Great Britain
by Amazon